Financial Life Plan

The Instruction Manual

C. J. Stegall-Evans

A. C. Evans

Editor

Mustard Seed Press

ISBN: 978-0-9897077-2-5

Dedicated to my father, Harold Stegall, and my mother, Odell Ramsey. Thank you for encouraging me to have a strong work ethic and to know the value of a dollar.

Failure is a matter of conceit; People don't work hard because, in their conceit, they imagine they'll succeed without ever making an effort. Most people believe they will wake up some day and find themselves rich. Actually, they've got it half right, because eventually they do wake up.

~Thomas Edison~

Foreword

Do you have a plan for your life? Are you allowing life to happen all around you with no rhyme or reason? It is often said, "You have to have a plan." It is rare that someone tells you what that plan is and how to go about creating it. Most people think, I've graduated high school or I have graduated college now what? Financial Life Plan gives you the fundamentals to help you create your financial life plan one step at a time. This will give you the breathing room to make informed decisions.

It does not matter your income level it is achievable. There is no big secret, this is a no nonsense, roll up your sleeves and get to work approach to acquiring and maintaining wealth. This is not a get rich quick scheme, but rather a map to put you on the road to financial stability.

This volume is intentionally brief, as it is an instruction manual, so that you may remember what you read and adapt it to fit your lifestyle. This book is less than 100 pages because 90% of readers never make it past the first chapter. Its cost is less than $10.00 so that it is affordable to all. I suggest you keep it on your nightstand or somewhere close to use as a reference and to keep you motivated. Now, get a cup of coffee, tea or something that sooths you and sit with me as I discuss financial literacy and as you decide what your future looks like and the concrete steps you need to take to get there. Please, enjoy the journey.

C. J. Stegall-Evans

Introduction

I was bedridden for a few weeks; I typically read a book a week but since I was in bed and I do not have a TV in my bedroom, I was downloading and binge reading book after book on my e-reader. My research for the last ten-plus years has been both educational and financial literacy. I have been racking my brain trying to find simple solutions to big problems. My primary problem was my inability to maintain wealth. Since I was studying educational and financial literacy simultaneously, it struck me that financial literacy is similar to educational literacy in that students struggle because they lack a strong foundation with which to build their skills upon.

I kept trying to figure out what was missing. In my financial literacy readings I kept running across the name of a little book: *The Richest Man in Babylon,* by George S. Clason. I thought, what can a man that was born in 1874 tell me about how to prosper in the 21st century? After reading the first page of his prose, it turns out everything.

I was so inspired I decided to take all the information I had gathered over the years and put it into a format that is accessible to all; because reading this little tome, along with all the other information I had gathered, was like getting struck by a bolt of lightning. I suddenly had the key that was missing from my financial literacy. I had all this educational know-how but lacked the foundational elements to pull it all together in a manner that motivated me to act upon it. So, for you, dear reader, as a collector of wisdom, I have put it all together so that you may avoid some major hiccups on the road to solvency.

A Part Of All You Earn Is Yours To Keep!

~George S. Clason~

I am sure most of us have heard "pay yourself first" nevertheless did we really hear and internalize it. If you start today saving just 10% of what you earn you will immediately begin to take on a wealth mentality. Saving 10% will be challenging for some because your purse does not, yet, know you are a wealthy person in the making. Be assured regardless of your income level this process is applicable to you. This 10% is yours to keep. It is not to loan out, buy clothes or indulge in anything. Its sole purpose is to go to work for you. This is your nest egg, the beginning of your fortune.

Anyone who may think they don't have enough to save 10%, then you especially should be saving 10%. This money is yours, not the government, not the hottest new designer, not your friends or even family. This money is your workhorse; as this money begins to add up and accumulate interest it begins to work for you. When you are older instead working harder, this is the money that will work hard for you.

It is not what you have right now that counts but what you will have in the future. If you follow no other rule in this book, by all means follow this one. This rule will immediately begin to make your money multiply. You have heard the saying, "It takes money to make money," well this is the money that is the foundation on which you build your wealth.

This is planting the seeds of your prosperity. It may not seem like much but this one act will ignite within you the determination you need to succeed. I don't know about you but when I am older I don't want to depend on social security to take care of me. Plus if you have the ability to take care of yourself you also get to choose your lifestyle.

How is this applicable?

This rule is applicable because we all need to start somewhere and this is the first step on the road to prosperity. This is an investment in yourself and your commitment to having the life you want. This puts you one step closer to owning your life. The 10% rule are not just words; this is a binding agreement with yourself that is to be honored with honesty and integrity. This is setting a solid financial foundation for yourself and future generations of your family.

Action Plan:

No matter what, save at least 10%. Remember the wise words of George Clason, "part of all you earn is yours to keep." No matter what your income level, if you don't have your own money, or if you are in debt, you are enslaved. Start your plan, now! Sit down and figure out how you can save at least 10%. If you are of modest means, that's okay, figure out something you can do without; I assure you it will be worth in the long run. The most interesting thing is when you begin to save 10% you don't miss it. Your future has to be more important than material things. Even a bit of discomfort is worth obeying the 10% rule.

Control Your Spending; It Is More Important To Have Money, Than To Look Like You Have Money

A few years back I was on a trip and guest were gathered in my hotel room. There were a pair of reading glasses on the desk next to my books. Someone asked, "*Whose glasses are these?*" Since they were next to my books I assumed they were mine. One of the guests spoke up and said they were not mine because they were Dolce and Gabbana. Everyone laughed knowing they were definitely not mine. I laughed too, because I did not want to wear Dolce and Gabbana, I wanted to be like Dolce and Gabbana. The last time I purchased reading glasses and they were in a pack of three on sale at Costco for $16.99.

Although, I do not have designer reading glasses; I am in a room with people who love me, having room service (one of my favorite indulgences), and eating some of those delicious Double Tree cookies. We owe it to ourselves as responsible consumers to choose those products and experiences that work for us. I absolutely have nothing against anyone else having Dolce and

Gabbana reading glasses, but it does not fit my lifestyle.

It is up to each of us to find what's important to us and our lifestyle then consciously become consumers of those things that truly brings us joy. There's so much to desire out there and advertisers are trying to relieve us of our hard earned money 24/7.

There's always the latest technology, the trendiest fashion, the sportiest car. We cannot have it all. It's just not possible. It is not expected that you give up all pleasures, simply choose judiciously. Look at the life you want to find out what's important to you. It is possible to have anything you want, but for most of us it is not possible to have everything we want.

If you want a luxurious life style with this process it is still attainable, but on the contrary, it would be prudent to practice delaying your gratification. Having savings has to become more important than having things. Freedom has to be more important than material possessions. If not, then you are a slave to your possessions. Your life and freedom are the most important things you possess. It should be more important to work to enjoy life than it is to work to have things. According to Henry David Thoreau, "My greatest skill in life is to want but little."

How is this applicable?

This is applicable because people and advertisers are always trying to part you from your money. It is so easy to make a spontaneous purchase without thought as to the consequences this will have on savings. The more you spend the less you save. Just like your savings will cumulatively grow as you add 10%, your debt will increase as you spend. If you are using credit cards, and not paying them off at the end of every month, then you are also spending your future earnings. You are making things more important than yourself.

Action Plan:

Become a conscious consumer. Live beneath your means. Take the time to think about how you want to spend your money. Do not spend money to fit in or influence how you want others to perceive you. Not being a voracious consumer is a habit worth cultivating. Focus on your debt for 30 days: other than groceries (necessary groceries) and essentials, do not spend those dollars for which you have worked so hard. You have worked too hard to simply give your money away. Do retailers deserve your money more than you? During this 30 days take the time to simplify your wants and curb your desires. Remember your money has a job to do; it has to support you. If you spend it all then your money is supporting someone else.

Do the Work

When I was in graduate school I took an education class called Measurements. In this class we worked together as a group and put together a weekly test booklet with standardized test questions (prompts). So, each week one person would be responsible for putting together the portfolio of test questions that other group members had emailed to him or her. I was a member of a lazy group, when my week came no one ever sent any prompts, so I ended up doing all the work.

My group was so irresponsible that one week when it wasn't my week to put the portfolio together my entire group showed up late with no portfolio. But, by then, I was so used to this group being unreliable that I started routinely putting together a test packet every week, to ensure that I get an A. In fact, when we initially started the project each person got to go up to the front of the class and get sample test portfolios so that we would know what kind of work we needed to produce. When it was my turn I was given two packets one with an A letter grade and the other a B. I gave the B portfolio back, because I didn't need to be instructed on how to make a B. Thus, this set the tone for the rest of the class for me.

I was at first so frustrated that I was in such a lethargic group I thought about telling the professor. But then I stopped and thought, *I am really enjoying this, plus I could ensure we get an A. On the other hand, if I told the professor I would not get to continue doing all the work.* I also had a sneaky suspicion that this group might have given me a million dollar idea.

Following this class I began to write prompts on my own to the very best of my ability. This led to me developing prompts that promote proficient writing for low achieving students. Those prompts have blossomed into *Word Nerd: An Intensive Writing Practice.* Presently these workbooks are being transformed into an effective writing and reading program that will become available to low achieving schools. So this group started a career path for me that I might not have had otherwise.

So don't be afraid to work hard, the unenterprising people around you are giving you a gift. They are giving you the opportunity to acquire more experience and skill. They just may be paving the way for a new career for you. Where there is work there is always opportunity, look for it and be prepared.

Since we spend so many hours at work, we might as well enjoy it. According to Dr. Martin Luther King, Jr., "If a man is called to be a street sweeper, he should sweep the streets as Michelangelo painted, or Beethoven composed music or Shakespeare wrote poetry. He should sweep the streets so well that all the host of heaven and earth will pause and say, *'Here lived a great street sweeper who did his job well'*."

Working with excellence has its benefits, although, I really didn't appreciate it at the time, my classmates were a blessing in disguise. What may look unfair can be transformed into a path to your future career. While on your path to greatness, I will lend one word of caution, remember to watch out for distractions.

That's right distractions; we live in the information age and so much and so many are vying for our attention. The internet, smart phone, TV and a host of other people and things. It easier than ever to put off any task at hand until tomorrow. Whenever you feel the urge to be entertained rather than work think of it this way: I am watching someone else work. The people I am watching on TV and the internet are doing their job and following their passion. There is no way I am going to put more effort into watching someone else fulfil their dreams, than my own. All this accessible entertainment robs you of your time and your life.

There is an old story by Mark Twain: A man meets St. Peter at the gates of heaven. He is a military history buff with a burning question. He asked, *"St. Peter, tell me who is the greatest general who ever lived?"* St. Peter points and says, *"That man over there."* The man asking the question looks puzzled and responds, *"How could he be the greatest general who ever lived? I knew that man in life he was a common laborer."* St. Peter responds, *"If he had been a general he would have been the greatest general who ever lived."*

Don't be an "if"; whatever you want to be in life you can achieve it. According to George Clason, "Where there is determination a way can be found." Love and trust yourself enough to find a way.

How is this applicable?

This is applicable because we all come into this world to serve a purpose. Our jobs (homemakers included) are how we care for our families. Our jobs are how we serve others. Our jobs are where we spend most our time and effort 40 hours or more a week. Our first jobs are just that a first job, we have to be ever on the lookout for better opportunities. No matter what the income level we still need to honor ourselves by saving 10%. Do your best on your job, not to satisfy your boss, but to esteem yourself. Work hard knowing that it may look like you are working for someone else but in actuality you are working for yourself. For now, don't worry about the job you have, all legal work is honorable work. No one outside of yourself can stand in the way of your success.

Action Plan:

Strive to do more than what is asked in your work. Know that every day brings you a step closer to where you want to be in life. Set your intention and make a goal as to where you want to go. Don't just think about it, write it down. Writing it down makes it real. Things written down become our goal especially if we have concrete steps to achieve said goal. If you don't yet know your goal or how to get to where you want to go in life then research, research, research. You are worth the time and effort.

Pay Your Debts

George Clason recommends saving 10% of your income, paying debts with 20% of your income and living on 70% of your income. This is wisdom no one can argue against. Since advertisements are overstimulating our senses 24 hours a day, it is easier now than at any other time in history to go deeply into debt.

There are more material possessions than any one person could possibly purchase. Consumers are constantly being sold things they never even knew they wanted. So with all these purchases the consequence of our actions can lead to huge debt. Add that to the regular consumer debts that we may have such as our homes, student loans, and transportation. It is so easy for it all to spin out of control and begin a downward spiral from which recovery seems impossible.

Conversely, once in debt there is only one way out, one step at a time. Clason admonishes us to pay off our debts as aggressively as possible. We are to pay off debts from 20% of our income. If you can dig into the 70% and pay off your debts more aggressively, great, but if not, never reach in and borrow from your 10%. Remember: This money has a job, it is working for you.

Call your creditors to make arrangements so that you devise a way to pay off your debt within the 20% of your income range. Although this may not be your creditors preferred method of repayment, something is better than nothing. This will allow you to pay off debt with dignity, have money to live on, and still have the money that is working for you.

How is this applicable?

This is applicable because the majority of us have one or more times spiraled deeply into debt. It is a hapless feeling when it seems all your money is being absorbed into the ether and you can't figure out how to start putting your life in order again.

Action Plan:

Make a repayment plan equaling 20% of your income. If your debts are more than your income payment range then make arrangements with your debtors. Deal with your debts honestly and with

Integrity; make a commitment to repayment, while living with as much ease as possible within your 70% living expenses and allowing your 10% to continue working for you.

Budget

Using 70% of your income make a budget. This budget is not to restrict you, but rather to make you free. Make a list of your essentials and those things that are important to your lifestyle. This is an opportunity to figure out what is truly important to you. Set a priority for what stays and what you are willing to give up to remain within your 70% budget range. For some this will be easy, for others this is quite the challenge. Think of it this way: You can play less now in order to play more, later. If you decide otherwise, playing more now may mean giving up a secure, calm and stable lifestyle that we desire as we get older. Playing more now is fun, but it has its consequences.

It is not suggested that you give up everything for the sake of your budget. Rather, think about your lifestyle in reference to your income and adjust it accordingly. Some will be shocked to discover they are living well above their means. Others will welcome the breathing room this act of frugality brings.

This is an opportunity to be honest with yourself about what you make and how you spend it. If you are doing this experiment with others in your social circle, remember, your budget need not look like theirs because your priorities may be different. If designer items are a part of your lifestyle by all means budget for it. For some having luxury items may mean saving a portion of their 70% to acquire it, this is fine, but never ever dip into your 10% savings because this money has a job. The minute you dip into your 10% your money stops working for you and you begin working for your money, or as Thoreau would say, "Men have become the tool of their tools." Money is a tool to make your life easier.

How is this applicable?

This is applicable because unless we are making millions a year for life most of us have a limit to our income. Having a budget allows for us to have the best possible life within that income limit. It eliminates stress and allows you to know where your money is going. It allows you to have more control over your life, while building a better future. A budget is not about restriction it's about honesty. When we are honest with ourselves we are able to face the world with more confidence. Because we have a budget and we have money that works for us 24/7 we are building a firm foundation for our financial future. Taking control of your finances means taking a deep breath and allowing the weight of the world to roll off your shoulders. It's about being kind to yourself and giving yourself the life you deserve. Pat yourself on the back, you are well on your way to a sound financial future.

Action Plan:

Sit down, have a cup of tea, coffee or something that sooths you. Think about your priorities. Include in your budget the essentials such as mortgage, rent, food, and utilities. Make a list of the non-essential items and cross out the things you can do without.

Tips:

- Take a look at you cable and wireless bills to ensure you are getting the best possible deals.

- Before you go to the grocery store, know what you are going to eat for the next week, make a list, and know how much you are willing to spend. Adhere to your list as much as possible. Be wary of isles with items not found on your list because you will find yourself wanting what you don't need. Additionally your grocer switches around the store items periodically, so that you will have to look for your item and perhaps make a spontaneous purchase. Do not give in to the good music and intoxicating smells. I was shocked to discover that paying a bit more attention and adhering to my grocery list saves me on average $200 per month.

- Be sure to balance your check book on a regular basis.

Take Wise Counsel

Now that this 10% is working for us we have to decide what to do with it. It's very easy to get lured in with high rates of return and dreams of getting rich quick. Unusually high rates of returns are deceitful and will cause those unaware to lose everything they own in chasing a dream; there really are no shortcuts. This book is based on the get rich slow principal because, unfortunately, getting rich quickly is a rare phenomenon. Those young rich people in the media are an anomaly. The average millionaire is 50-plus when they make their first million. When I told this to my former students I saw disappointed faces and heard *"but Ms. Evans 50 is so old."* The truth is time will pass whether or not you follow your dreams. Even if you are trying to get rich quick it would still be wise to ensure in the coming years you have modest returns and that your money is secure.

It is better to allow your money to sit in a bank account with meager earnings than to put it into a vehicle that promises high rates of return only to lose most or all of your money. That is why it's imperative that we take wise counsel. Clason relates the following story to prove that point:

In *The Richest Man in Babylon,* there is a parable about a scribe who is under the wise counsel of his financial mentor. The mentor visits him periodically to see how the scribe is managing his 10%. Once after a two-year absence the mentor returns to see how this young scribe is doing. The scribe tells the mentor that he has given his money to a brick maker to travel overseas to buy rare jewels. And when the brick maker comes back he will sell all the jewels, get high rates of returns and they will divide the earnings. The mentor tells the young scribe "*advice is the one thing that is freely given away, but watch that you take only what is worth having.*" He reminds him to only take advice from those who are experienced in such matters. When the brick maker returns they discovered he purchased worthless bits of glass that look like jewels. The scribe learns a wise lesson but at the high cost of all his savings.

I too, have learned this lesson the hard way, as I have lost everything in the stock market, twice. So, as a rule, I don't invest in individual stocks. I am a passive investor who invest across as the stock market index. My money is relatively safe and my rates of return are modest (I am not a stockbroker, or skilled in the stock market). I find investing in index funds to be a method that works for me. You will have to seek wise counsel, do your homework and find what works best for you. This is not an endorsement of index funds this is simply me telling you how I invest my money. You may be someone who is willing to take more risk than myself, but be careful. There are far too many people in this world willing to help you part with your money. Remember, you are the only one responsible for your financial security.

We will find in life those always willing to give us advice it is incumbent upon each of us to consider the source. Clason urges us to cultivate our own powers to study, become wiser, and skilled as to respect ourselves. In this way we can be confident that we are making wise decisions.

There will be hiccups on your road to wealth, and lessons to be learned. Be open to the lessons, try not to make the same mistake twice. But whatever you do don't give up, mediocrity is for other people.

How is this applicable?

This is applicable because few can resist a deal that seems too good to be true. The problem is if it's too good to be true, it usually is. Therefore, whenever we invest our money ensure that the broker or whomever is our wise counsel has the skill and/or education to help us make an informed decision.

Action Plan:

If you're just starting out, keep your 10% in the bank and begin to explore other areas for higher but not risky rates of return. This will take a bit of homework on your part, but it's your money and no one else has more of a vested interest in your finances than you.

Make Your Money Work for You

According to George Clason, making your money work for you is "the first step leading to the temple of wealth, and no man may climb higher who cannot plant his feet firmly on the first step." Your financial success is not something outside of yourself. Your financial success begins with you. If the government gets their percentage of your money without fail there is no reason you should not get yours without fail.

I know I've touched on "making your money work for you" many times within this book. There's a reason for that: I want to make sure you and your subconscious knows that this is a necessary step on your road to wealth. If at any time you decide to dip into your 10%, I want the red flashing light of your subconscious to come on, I want the alarm to sound loudly, and your inner voice to scream, "Danger, Will Robinson!!!"

I want there to be no doubt whatsoever that of part of what you earn is yours to keep. I want there to be no doubt whatsoever that this money has a job to do. This money's job is to work for you. This money's job is to take care of you. To spend the money that supposed to work hard and take care of you is disrespectful to yourself.

How is this applicable?

This is applicable because you have to make yourself a priority. Your future is not in the hands of someone else. Your success or failure depends on no one else but you. You have to give yourself the opportunity to be successful in life. To be accomplished you have to start somewhere and this is the first step; as Mr. Clason said, "no man may climb higher without his feet planted firmly on the first step." Saving 10% may seem like such a simple thing and it is; where there is simplicity there is truth.

Action Plan:

Recommit to saving at least 10% of everything you earn. This practice is not for a day, a month, a year but for a lifetime. This simple discipline has the ability to change your life. If you do nothing else in this book, acquire this habit and make your money work for you. When your money is working for you, it gains interest and that interest gains interest as this is happening you are continually adding the 10% continually gaining interest and the cumulative effect is great wealth. If your money is working for you, this makes your future a lot easier.

Educate Yourself

Since no one has more of a vested interest in your financial future than you it is imperative that you educate yourself. This may mean going back to school and getting a degree and/or taking full advantage of the fact that we live in the information age and can self-educate. There are so many opportunities for self-education at everyone's fingertips; there is absolutely no excuse not to be knowledgeable in your field or have some area of expertise. I am aware that some may not have easy access to computers but you have to find a way to educate yourself because companies have no qualms about sending jobs to countries where the labor is cheaper. Educating yourself puts you in a position to have more control over your life.

Educating oneself is important because those who are wealthy typically read at least 20 minutes a day. So while you are squirreling away your 10%, you also have to make another investment in yourself. Educating yourself ensures that you don't become stagnant and that you have the ability to move forward to a more meaningful life. Education makes you more beneficial to the company you work for and makes you more knowledgeable so that you may start your own business. This all begins with education, and learning the guidelines of what it takes to become successful.

The best way to learn to be successful is to learn from successful people. If you cannot find a personal mentor, there are all kinds of books and internet articles with accomplished people providing a road map of their journey to affluence. Your journey may not look like theirs but in educating yourself you will get ideas. Ideas brought to fruition are just as good as money in the bank. Everything you touch and use on a daily basis started with an idea. The more informed you are the better your ideas and your capacity to make knowledgeable decisions based on accurate information.

How is this applicable?

This is applicable because we live in the information age and knowledge is power. This is beneficial to help you feel more confident with yourself and in your work environment. Educating yourself is not about arrogance, rather, having knowledge or knowing where to go to get the information allows you to make informed decisions.

Education is adding significance to yourself and your work environment. Information is money in the bank and employers hire educated/skilled workers because they know they are trainable. It becomes easier to climb higher within your work place if you are adding value. If you are not being promoted or have a dead-end job, no worries, you are still adding significantly to your wealth of knowledge. You are learning and training yourself for bigger and better things. You are preparing to promote yourself. If you have already taken this step congratulations you are way ahead of the game.

Action Plan:

Start today, becoming a lifelong learner. If you are not already a reader start reading informative material five to ten minutes a day, and work your way up to 20 to 30 minutes a day. If you do not care for reading, remember, it is a habit like any other. The more you read the better you become, and the more you like it. E-readers make it easier than ever as they make it quick and effortless to find definitions as you discover new words. If you don't have much time to read, listen to an audio book in your down time or in your car.

Tips:

- Strive to learn more about your finances and your area of expertise.
- Ensure that you are well read and know more about your job than anyone around you.
- Endeavor to become the go to person in your office or work environment.

Promote Yourself: Solve a Problem

Education enriches almost every aspect of your life and enhances your potential for growth. We all know growing pains aren't always easy. Begin growing right where you are, while with your current employer start educating yourself. This will enable you to become an invaluable part of your organization. Additionally, become a problem solver. If there is a problem within your home or your work environment, sit down and figure a way to solve it. Those who solve problems give themselves a job.

In fact, this book came about as a result of a problem. I work really hard and I have more than one stream of income, however I still could not figure out my inability to increase/maintain my wealth. Then I went back and started doing what my father told me years ago I began saving at least 10%. Just that little tweak immediately changed everything. It felt like a magic, as if overnight I went from clueless to becoming more financially comfortable with each passing day. I had this workhorse that began working for me. Since I had a workhorse working for me I could began to work on other things.

Hence, I began to focus on my work rather than my income. I set up my budget so that a large portion of my income goes back into my business because I do not wish to incur loans. As a result, I live on a small portion of my 70% budget. Yet, I feel rich because I get up every morning and do what I love for a living.

Therefore, since I'm saving at least 10% and doing what I love one of the other things I began working on is this book. After reading *The Richest Man in Babylon* I was so inspired by Clason's work that the words for this book simply poured like water from my fingertips. I know this was figuratively but felt literal, as if words were actually pouring from my fingertips. I was so sick I could barely move but I had to prop myself up on pillows so I could write.

Although I was in agony, I also saw this as an opportunity to solve a problem and promote myself. Opportunities do not always come at convenient times but they do come. So be prepared when an opportunity is at your fingertips, because it may just be from inspiration born in 1874.

You see, after reading *The Richest Man in Babylon* and getting a different viewpoint on things I already knew. I decided that if I didn't quite have my financial and career plans in order there are others out there like me who could also benefit from this knowledge.

Thus, when we solve a problem for ourselves and those around us we benefit both ourselves and our community. When we learn something teaching it to others reinforces it within ourselves. Also when we help others we help ourselves because the energy we put into the world is the energy we get back.

How is this applicable?

This is applicable because there are problems all around us just waiting for someone like you to solve. Solving this problem could put you on a new career path, and/or the gateway to creating wealth. Don't be someone watching TV and saying, "I had that idea years ago but I didn't act on it." If not acted upon, unsolved problems go on to the next person who is willing and open to filling this job. It is said, "Necessity is the mother of invention;" it is also opportunity knocking loudly.

Action Plan:

Become aware of the world around you. Look for ways in which you can make it better. Look for ways in which you can build a better mousetrap. It will become more important in the future to have an area of expertise or a niche service you can provide via the internet or within your community. We have to be open to growth and change because the job market as we know it is changing every year. Pay attention, and see how you can add value to your home, work, or community environment. When a problem arises, don't just let it go, that's opportunity knocking on your door. Be prepared when opportunity comes because it may look different than expected.

Tip:

- This is an original work in spired by The Richest Man in Babylon. Although Mr. Clason presents these lessons in the form of a parables, I simply gave you straightforward information in a no-nonsense format that may be applied to your life. I updated a few of his suggestions, and added a few things that reflects the time in which we live. I hope you still read *The Richest Man in Babylon,* as I think they work well as companion books, and as an interesting prospective across the century.

Confidence

What would it mean to have the ability to be yourself in a world that tells you who you should be? We all come into this life so full of genius. Somewhere along the way, well-meaning people take a look at us, and figure out who we should be, and slowly begin to mold us into that form. Fortunately for me I had a saving grace:

When I was five years old and I was looking out over my grandmother's garden greeting the sunrise. I held my head up to the sun like a flower receiving radiant energy. In this moment it was put into my heart that I was a flower like all the others in the garden. All the flowers are different, all the flowers are beautiful. Some may not be able to see your beauty, but you are still a flower.

I am a flower and so are you, dear friend. Additionally, as flowers we are all lovely in our own way and different. In as much as I am flower I can appreciate the strength, intelligence, and beauty of other flowers. Dear Flower, began to cherish yourself and those around you. We have to choose the words we use with ourselves and others wisely so as not to plant weeds in our garden.

Just like we can use words to build people up, we can also use words to tear people down. So we need to be careful what we say, but we also need to put distance between ourselves and those who use words to try and make us feel inferior.

Life is beautiful, do not surround yourself with people who cannot see it that way, because they want to destroy your confidence in order to enhance their own. They are trying take away what makes you a flower like none other.

However, it is ourselves who are ultimately responsible for who we are and who we will become. I am aware that this little book is simple but packs a powerful punch. For some who take the challenge it is some small changes and a few tweaks. For others it will mean looking at the world in a different light and making necessary changes for growth and prosperity. Usually, nothing worthwhile is easy. It takes courage and confidence just to get through our everyday lives. It takes even more when we decide to stretch beyond the constraints of our comfort zone and attempt to be more than we thought possible.

On your journey toward prosperity you will encounter many obstacles. These barriers are life's attempt to see how badly you want that in which you are pursuing. The road to your dream may at some point become long and lonely. You may discover those who you thought had your back are nowhere to be found. Some days you may be your only cheerleader.

By all means, be your greatest cheerleader. In our childhood there are those of us who heard the negative voices coming from both adults and children telling us we are not special, or in some way not good enough. Asking us, "*who do you think you are*?" These negative voices have a way of undermining our perception of ourselves. After a while others don't have to do this anymore because we take on the negative self-talk and began to undermine our own purpose.

Others of us are told we are precious and beautiful and felt the need to be perfect and pleasing to others. No one can be perfect and no one should bend themselves out of place trying to please others. Trying to live up to a perfect image, especially when your self-talk says otherwise is an impossible task. How do we change this? How do we become our biggest cheerleaders?

We start by letting go of the negative baggage of the past. We start by remembering that we have a purpose in this life and is our duty to find out what that is and contributed that to society. We start with replacing the negative self-talk with positive self-talk. When we hear our self say, "I can't do it" we interrupt and say, "I will do it."

We start by being as kind to ourselves in private, as we are to others in public. We start by appreciating our best qualities and accepting our flaws, knowing that we are a work in progress trying to improve one day at a time. We start by reading positive quotes every day, or having a positive affirmation. We start by reading or listening to a motivational message every day until we are motivated.

There is no time to point fingers, we need to meditate and/or pray, journal, get psychological help, or do whatever is necessary to let it go. Others only have the power that we give them. This is baggage we can no longer afford to carry, it's too heavy, and it's too expensive. This book is only a starting point it is up to the individual to do the heavy lifting.

How is this applicable?

There is no way to effect change without effort. The moment we begin to make positive changes we run into roadblocks. These hurdles are there to see what we are made of, to see how high we are willing to jump; and if we will give up or persevere. Sometimes our single biggest obstruction is ourselves, therefore we need to change the way we speak to ourselves. We need to be kinder and dig deep to discover who we really are. In a world full of so much information and so many messages from people and the media and so many other things outside of ourselves it's easy to get lost or disconnected. Being positive and getting to know ourselves gives us the confidence to know that we truly do have the ability to do anything.

Action Plan:

Take time every day to recharge and focus on the positive things in life. Spend at least five minutes every day quietly with yourself. According to Blaise Pascal, "All of humanity's problems stem from man's inability to sit quietly in a room alone." Additionally read something positive every day. Try to write something positive on a daily basis, you will be amazed at your ability to write your world right. Writing keeps us honest and positive.

Our goal should be to embody the ancient wisdom of Lao Tzu:

Because one believes in oneself,

One doesn't need to convince others.

Because one is content with oneself,

One does not need others approval.

Because one accepts oneself,

The whole world accepts him or her.

Gratitude

Life is a gift and we should treat it as such. None of us know, what comes beyond this life. Even those who profess to know, honestly don't know for sure. So we need to take time every day to be grateful for our life past, present, and future. We have to be grateful for what we have now so that we can fully appreciate what we will have in the future.

We have to be grateful for what we have right now so that we can go on to the next phase of our lives. We need to allow time to be present, look around and actually stop and say "thank you." When we are grateful there is little room for hate, frustration and other negative emotions. It allows us to be open to creativity, and reach beyond our perceived ability.

Gratitude allows us to be humble so that we may carry out our purpose in a manner that does not demean or hurt ourselves or others. It means being an open vessel to all life has to offer. Gratitude is about love. Love for oneself, and love for one's fellow human beings. Like most things in life, if gratitude is not naturally inherent in us, it will takes practice. But it is a practice that fills us with love, joy, and creativity.

You may ask, what gratitude has to do with creating wealth? Creating wealth is not about just getting rich, although you will, if that is your desire. Creating wealth is having the ability to own one's life. Creating wealth is about fulfilling your purpose in serving humanity in the job you were put on earth to do. In my book, that is absolutely something that fills one with gratitude.

How is this applicable?

This is applicable because wealth alone cannot make one happy. Finding your purpose and doing it to the best of your ability is wealth creation of the highest order. Creating wealth with nothing meaningful to show for it is often fleeting and empty. In creating wealth we should do so in a manner that contributes something amazing to the world. This is the kind of riches worth striving to achieve. Don't just make yourself rich make the world a richer place because you are here.

Action Plan:

Take some time every day to cultivate gratitude. Watch a sunrise or sunset, read a poem. We have this remarkable thing called life, we can live it in wonder and awe to all that is around us.

We also cultivate gratitude by helping others. We can help others with our time, our money, by doing whatever we possibly can to lift someone else up. There are so many different ways to be of service. When we help others we are not only benefiting them but we are also building our confidence, joy and overall wellbeing.

Epilogue

This book is but an outline of a plan to create financial stability. The road you take is up to you. Use this as a model and create your own plan specific to your station in life and where you want to go. Remember, your plan will not all come together exactly as written chapter and verse. The important thing is not to give up. It is said, "Those who do not plan, are planning to fail."

Take some time, sit down, think about your life, and how you want to live it. According to Plato, "The life which is unexamined is not worth living." Life is short and difficult to maneuver with no thought or plan. Consequently, far too many people are trying to get to the top without first laying a firm foundation.

If you are waiting for the perfect time to begin this journey: There is no perfect time. There is only time and the clock will continue ticking whether or not you undertake this venture. If you allow it something will always get in your way. Don't let that something be you. Although, fulfilling your dreams will not be easy, once you set your intention, and write down your plan the Universe will move heaven and earth to help you achieve it. The world is waiting for you to discover your genius. Dig in, do the work, and surprise us.

Acknowledgements

Thank you so very much to my editor and son, A. C. Evans. Your talent as both a writer and editor are invaluable.

About the Author

C. J. Stegall-Evans is a Writer and Educational Consultant who lives in North Florida. She has a M.A. in English Language Arts Education and an additional majors in Professional Writing and Community College Teaching. Her undergraduate degree is in Religious Studies. Blog: www.writingasasacredart.com.

Other Books by C. J. Stegall-Evans

The Elements of Faith: 40 Faith and Confidence Building Meditations

Textbook series by C. J. Stegall-Evans and A. C. Evans

Word Nerd: An Intensive Writing Practice

Made in the USA
Monee, IL
04 November 2026

67375688R00039